CONTENTS

The Devil's Marbles, p.35

WHAT'S HOT: AUSTRALIA

Big Day Out festival, p.20

Australia is the world's sixth-largest country, and the only country that's also a continent. It's so big that whatever kind of activity you're looking for – whether you're a sports nut, a culture-vulture, or a beach lover – there's a good chance you will find it in Australia. Here are just a few of the highlights you can find out about later in the book.

1. TAKE A FERRY AROUND SYDNEY HARBOUR p.12

Sydney Harbour has 240 km of shoreline, dotted by smart houses, docks and nature reserves. One of the best ways to see it is to take a public ferry from Circular Quay in the heart of the city.

2. SWIM AT ST KILDA p.14

The elegant old spa resort in one of Melbourne's inner suburbs is a great place to soak up a bit of Australia's Victorian heritage – and to have a soak in the indoor heated seawater pool.

3. PILE INTO A BRONTE BEACH BARBECUE p.18

Sunday barbecues are an Australian tradition. As four in every five people live within an hour's drive of the beach, that's where they often take place.

4. HAVE A BIG DAY OUT p.20

The biggest music festival in Australia, Big Day Out, happens in January and features bands from around the world. The festival travels around the country, visiting major cities.

5. LEARN TO SURF AT THE BIRTHPLACE OF SURFING p.26

Australians were introduced to surfing in December 1915, at Freshwater Beach, Sydney, when Hawaiian swimming champion Duke Kahanamoku gave a demonstration. It's an historical place to catch your first wave!

6. BREATHE IN THE FUMES OF THE BATHURST 1000 p.30

Australia's biggest motorsports event features cars very like the one your parents drive – but these have been souped up, and spend six hours careering around the race circuit at speeds of up to 300 kph.

7. GO CAMPING WITH THE WUGULARR p.33

One weekend a year, the Wugularr Aboriginal people invite a small group onto their land deep in the Northern Territory. Once there, the guests experience Wugularr culture – traditional ceremonies, dances and performances few non-Wugularr have ever seen – before falling asleep beside a campfire.

Australians love the beach and the sea.

IT'S (NEARLY) OFFICIAL!
TOP PLACES TO VISIT IN AUSTRALIA

Members of one of the world's biggest travel websites picked these top Aussie destinations:

1. Sydney – the Sydney Festival in January is a big highlight, but this is a great place to visit at any time of the year

2. Melbourne – great restaurants and cafés, a lively music scene and loads of big sports events

3. Port Douglas – famous for two things: food and the Great Barrier Reef, one of the world's natural wonders

4. Cairns – welcomes adrenaline junkies, divers and people who want to explore the tropical north

5. Brisbane – this thriving, busy city is great if you like the beach life and warm weather

6. Byron Bay – in the 1970s a hippy-and-surfer hangout, now a chic seaside resort, Byron is a great place for surfing, yoga, live music and alternative therapies

AUSTRALIA FACTS AND STATS

The Blue Mountains

Australia has an amazing variety of things to see and do. You can pick your way through dense rainforest, surf giant waves, mountain bike along winding mountain paths... or just hang out eating ice cream at a pavement café.

LANDSCAPE

Australia has almost every kind of landscape you can imagine (and some you can't). Highlights to watch out for include:

- Gorges, pools and caves in the Bungle Bungles

- The Lost-World style escarpment of the Blue Mountains (above)

- Vast deserts (and underground towns, where people shelter from the heat) in South Australia

- The Great Barrier Reef, regularly voted one of the top wonders of the natural world

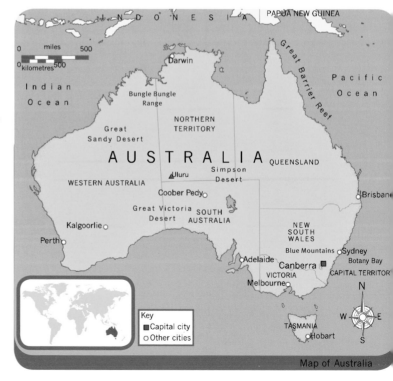

Key
■ Capital city
○ Other cities

Map of Australia

CLIMATE

The climate is mostly dry and hot. However, Australia is a huge country, and there are big variations. In the far north the climate is tropical, with dripping rainforests and wetland (watch out for the crocodiles!). In the south, the weather is sometimes cold and wet – heading south from Tasmania, the next stop is Antarctica.

The sun and heat mean travellers have to be careful to drink plenty, so that they don't get dehydrated. It's also important to wear high-factor sunscreen. The Australian sun is very strong, and in the past there were high rates of skin cancer among locals. These days, people are better informed about protecting their skin, so cancer rates have decreased.

Australia's hot, dry climate is the reason behind one of the country's biggest natural dangers: bushfires. These are a serious risk in areas where the vegetation has been dried out by long hot spells. Always pay heed to bushfire warnings: in the past, travellers have been caught in them and have died.

Kings Canyon, Northern Territory

FACT FILE ONE

CAPITAL CITY: Canberra

AREA: 7,682,300 km² (land territory), plus 58,920 km² (ocean territory)

HIGHEST MOUNTAIN: Mount Kosciuszko (2,229 m)

LOWEST POINT: Lake Eyre (15 m below sea level)

LONGEST RIVER: Murray (2,508 km)

BORDERS: Australia is a country, island and continent: it does not share borders with any other country

NATURAL HAZARDS: cyclones, bushfires, drought and deadly animals (see pages 36–37!)

PEOPLE

The first Australians were the Aborigines.

They had been living in Australia for tens of thousands of years when Europeans arrived in 1788. Since then, wave after wave of immigrants have settled in Australia. First came English, Irish, Welsh and Scots. Then Greeks, Turks, Polish and other European peoples followed. More recently, many immigrants have come from Southeast Asia or the Middle East.

Thai Songkran festival, Melbourne

Centre Place laneway, Melbourne

URBAN LIFE

Most Australians live in cities. In the city centres, apartment living is popular. People enjoy being able to walk out of the door and be near to cafés, sports facilities, shops, restaurants, cinemas, concert venues and all the other city attractions.

Further from the city centres, most people live in houses. Usually these have gardens, and often a swimming pool. There's plenty of space, but the downside is that the drive to work or school can take a long time.

RURAL LIFE

Coastal rural areas have become popular with wealthy Australians looking for peace and quiet near the beach. Many coastal areas of New South Wales, Queensland and Victoria are expensive places to live. Further inland, most rural settlements depend on mining or agriculture. In the tough interior landscapes, life is harder than in the cities. The distances between settlements can make for long journeys from place to place.

Coober Pedy, opal-mining town, South Australia

"With the exception of [Aboriginal] peoples, we are a nation of boat people whose forbears made the journey from elsewhere to our shores."

— Arnold Zable, Australian storyteller and writer

FACT FILE TWO

POPULATION: 22 million

POPULATION: Sydney (4.43 million), Melbourne (3.85 million), Brisbane (1.97 million), Perth (1.6 million)

AGE STRUCTURE: 18.2% under 15 years old; 67.5% 15–64 years old; 14.4% over 64 years old

YOUTH UNEMPLOYMENT (15–24 year-olds): 11.6%

OBESITY: 16.4%

LANGUAGES: English is by far the most widely spoken language. Small numbers of people also speak Chinese, Greek, Arabic and Vietnamese and Aboriginal languages

RELIGIONS: Christian (64%), Buddhist (2%), Muslim (2%)

SYDNEY

Sydney is close to where the first-ever European settlers landed in Australia. Today the city is still welcoming new arrivals. These days, though, they step off aeroplanes instead of sailing ships.

• •

SYDNEY FERRY/BUS/WALKING TOUR

Most people have a long plane journey to get to Australia – from Europe it takes about 24 hours of travelling. What better way to stretch your legs after the flight than a tour of the city?

1. Circular Quay to Watson's Bay

Start at Circular Quay, from where ferries fan out across Sydney Harbour. Catch the Watson's Bay ferry from Wharf 4. The harbour is regularly voted one of the most beautiful in the world, and this ferry ride is the perfect way to see it.

2. Watson's Bay to North Bondi

Take some time to explore the Watson's Bay area, before catching a bus to North Bondi. On your left will be the Tasman Sea, where the Pacific Ocean and Australia meet.

3. Bondi Beach to Bronte Beach

Drop down to the beach at Bondi, one of the world's most famous stretches of sand.

From here, take the cliff-top path south to Bronte Beach. On your way you pass Tamarama Beach – known as Glamarama because of the trendies who hang out there. It's a great place to stop for a drink.

The path continues past more beaches, but this is only your first day. It might be best to catch the bus back to the city centre!

Bondi to Bronte coastal walk

CITIES

SYDNEY
AUSTRALIA'S FIRST CITY

Founded: 1788

Population: 4.43 million (20% of all Australians)

Average age: 35

FESTIVALS

The Sydney Festival (January): for music, dance and drama

Vivid (May): uses light to give Sydney landmarks a new appearance at night

Sydney Film Festival (June): new movies from Australia and around the world

Climbing the Sydney Harbour Bridge

SYDNEY HIGHLIGHTS

1. The Sydney Bridge Walk
Climbing around the ironwork of the Sydney Harbour Bridge is quite a buzz!

2. Surf at Freshwater Beach
Catch the ferry to Manly and head for Freshwater for a surf lesson.

3. Visit Luna Park
The last remaining funfair in Sydney is right under the Harbour Bridge.

MELBOURNE

Melbourne at sunset

Melbourne and Sydney are fierce rivals. When Australia's different states united into one independent country in 1901, neither city would let the other be capital. In the end a whole NEW city, Canberra, had to be built.

MELBOURNE: AN INSIDER GUIDE

To find the Melbourne locals love, catch a tram to one of the city's inner suburbs. Here are some insider picks:

Richmond

Chow down on Greek food, Vietnamese feasts or fresh pizza before heading to the Corner Hotel, where there's live music three times a week.

Prahran

You can buy anything from snacks and cakes to locally made Ugg boots at Prahran's covered market. Then head over to Greville Street to check out the vintage stores.

Footscray

Footscray is an immigrant area and the markets here are full of the smells of Asia and Africa. Footscray is good for spices. If you want Vietnamese foods head to Footscray's Little Saigon Markets.

St Kilda

Top pick here is the St Kilda Sea Baths. They were built when open-air swimming was forbidden during daylight, as it was thought too rude. Today, you can still swim in a heated indoor seawater pool – great on cold days!

MELBOURNE AND THE GOLD RUSH

In 1851, gold was discovered near Melbourne. Gold diggers flocked to the area and Melbourne quadrupled in size within months. By 1865 it had become the biggest city in Australia. By the 1880s, Melbourne was said to be world's richest city.

THE GREAT OCEAN ROAD

West of Melbourne is the town of Torquay. This is the start of the Great Ocean Road, which is regularly voted one of the world's most beautiful roads. Built by returning soldiers after World War One (1914–18), it runs 243 km along the southern coastline.

COFFEE WARS

A barista is an expert coffee maker. Every year, Sydney and Melbourne have a contest to see which city has the best barista!

The Great Ocean Road

FOOD AND THE AUSSIE MELTING POT

The different peoples who have come to Australia over the years – Europeans, Pacific Islanders and Asians – have each brought their own styles of food and ingredients.

TRADITIONAL AUSTRALIAN TREATS

Every survey of Australia's favourite traditional foods includes deep-fried fish and chips, dagwood dog (a deep-fried, battered hotdog on a stick), chico rolls (giant, deep-fried spring rolls), and cheese-and-bacon roll (bread roll topped with cheese and bacon). Unfortunately, eating this kind of food comes at a cost! In 2012, it was reported that 63.25% of Australians were overweight.

FOODS YOU MIGHT NOT WANT TO TRY

1. Witchetty grub
They look like giant maggots, and you eat them alive – eew. If you can force one down, though, they actually taste good!

2. Green ant shake
Green ants and their larvae pounded to paste, then mixed with water? Apparently it makes a healthy, lemony drink.

3. Gould's goanna
A large lizard, traditionally cooked whole on the embers of a fire. People say it tastes like chicken.

FUSION FOOD

Today, many top Australian chefs combine Asian and Pacific Island flavours and styles with European cooking. This is called fusion food. It relies on simple recipes and fresh ingredients. Examples include lemongrass-and-lime chicken burgers, steamed fish with black-bean sauce, and caramelised wallaby tail with plum sauce.

EATING OUT

Eating out is a popular activity and there is a huge choice. The warm climate makes outdoor eating a pleasure, and in the evenings the city pavements are often crowded with diners.

Inside one of Sydney's top fusion restaurants

TOP STREET FOOD

Australia is a great place for street food. These are a few local favourites:

Meat pie: traditionally smothered in 'red sauce' (tomato ketchup). If you're hungry, a 'pie floater' is an upside-down pie in a bowl of pea soup.

Hamburger: in Australia, they serve hamburgers with beetroot. Even more surprising, it tastes good!

Souvlaki: a Greek kebab, meat and vegetables grilled on a skewer, then served in pitta bread.

Turkish pizza: thin pizza that can be rolled into a tube before eating.

SUNDAY BEACH BARBIES

In Australia, a Sunday barbecue is the equivalent of a roast lunch in Britain. Many parks and beauty spots have public electric barbecues, which cost just a few cents to use.

BRONTE BEACH BARBIE

One of the most popular Sydney spots for a barbecue at the beach is Bronte. What do you need to bear in mind if you want to join in the Sunday fun?

1. Get there early

This is a popular Sunday hangout, so arrive before midday to get a shady spot!

2. Bring plenty of coins

The public barbecues are coin-operated. There's nothing worse than running out of change before your sausages have even started to sizzle!

3. Cooking etiquette

You're expected to clean the barbecue once you have finished using it. Wandering off and pretending it's not your job will NOT be tolerated!

4. Bring your surfboard

Bronte often has good waves. Or if you're feeling lazy after lunch, there's a seawater pool to float around in.

THE LANGUAGE OF AUSSIE BARBECUES

Here are a few alternative barbecue food names:

Balmain bug: type of small lobster

Bangers, dodgers or snags: sausages

Chook: chicken

Flake: shark meat

Mudbug: crayfish

Yabby: freshwater crayfish

TOP BARBIE SPOTS

These are three great places for a barbecue or picnic (barbecues are not allowed in many rural areas, because of the risk of bushfires):

1. Marine Parade, Snapper Rocks, Queensland
Fill the time while your 'snags' (see panel on page 18) are cooking by watching the surfing action at one of Australia's top breaks.

2. Heathcote Reserve, Perth
High on a hill, this park has some of the best views of Perth and the Swan River.

3. One Tree Hill Picnic Ground, Victoria
You can hike to the picnic area along Fern Tree Gully, a very beautiful path. Be warned though: it's a steep walk with over 1,000 steps up!

Busy public barbecues on the seafront at Cairns, Queensland

MUSIC FESTIVALS

Huge crowd at the Big Day Out

Music festivals are popular in Australia. There are basically two kinds: big festivals with international stars as headliners and smaller festivals featuring local musicians.

BIG DAY OUT

Big Day Out is DEFINITELY a big, international-act kind of festival. In fact, it's one of the biggest festivals in Australia. It takes place in January, in the middle of summer, and sells out far in advance. The main stages often feature rock acts, while dance and electronic music fans head for the Boiler Room.

Unlike most festivals in Europe, Big Day Out isn't based in only one location. Each year it moves from Sydney to the Gold Coast, Adelaide, Melbourne and Perth. Most of the bands play at all the locations, so the festival is like a massive tour. Australian festivals often do this, so that bands travelling from far away can be seen by people in different parts of the country.

> "Big Day Out couldn't have been better. We spent the day eating ice cream, drinking gallons of water, drenching ourselves in sprinklers and dancing to some awesome DJs."
>
> — 2012 Big Day Out festival-goer

AUSTRALIAN FESTIVAL PLANNER

Here are some of the best music festivals in Australia:

JANUARY:

Field Day
(Sydney)

Field Day majors on dance music, and is held on New Year's Day in The Domain, a beautiful public park beside Sydney Harbour.

FEBRUARY/MARCH:

Soundwave
(various locations)

One for the metalheads, regularly featuring A-list acts such as Nine Inch Nails, Metallica and Blink 182.

JULY:

Splendour in the Grass
(Byron Bay)

Listen to a blend of rock, electronic, hip-hop and more as the waves crash gently on the shore. (The granola breakfasts, hair plaiting and yoga are optional.)

DECEMBER:

Homebake
(various locations)

This all-Australian music festival is incredibly popular: tickets sometimes sell out within ten minutes of being released.

Splendour in the Grass

CULTURE-VULTURE FESTIVALS

If you're the kind of culture-vulture who likes to swoop on **movies,** theatre, dance or comedy, there are plenty of festivals for you around Australia. One of the biggest and best happens in Adelaide, South Australia.

A street performer in front of the Rundle Mall Spheres, Adelaide

ADELAIDE FESTIVAL

The main Adelaide Festival is quite highbrow, with opera, theatre, classical music and dance performances. Alongside it, though, are two alternative festivals:

WOMADelaide

Features some of the biggest stars in world music. Previous big acts have included reggae legend Jimmy Cliff, early rap innovator Gil Scott Heron and the Malian megastar Salif Keita.

Adelaide Fringe

The Fringe begins with a free opening-night party, including a street parade. After that, you never know what kind of event you might bump into round the corner (or down a back alley, in an old warehouse or inside a disused building). It could be circus performers, dance, street theatre, comedy or a puppet show. The whole of the old city centre comes alive with all kinds of freaky shows!

LIGHT'S VISION

Adelaide's streets are laid out in a grid designed by the city's first Surveyor General, William Light. There are open squares in the centre, and parkland around the edges. It's the perfect layout for a festival city!

During the Sydney Festival, a giant screen rises from the harbour

CULTURE-VULTURE CALENDAR

JANUARY:

Sydney Festival
(New South Wales)

Dance, music, theatre, comedy, film and lots of free outdoor events.

MARCH:

Ten Days On The Island
(Tasmania)

The festival focuses on Tasmanian arts, from food to theatre, but also features performances by international artists.

AUGUST:

Darwin Festival
(Northern Territory)

The festival features cabaret, dance, music, film and more. It's an excellent place to see performances by Aboriginal Australians and Pacific Islanders.

AUGUST:

Melbourne* Film Festival
(Victoria)

The biggest film festival in Australia, where it would be impossible to see everything: the festival shows roughly 400 films from 50 countries.

*Melbourne film trivia: this is where the first feature-length film, The Story of the Kelly Gang, was shown in 1906.

BEACH LIFE

I n general, Aussies love the beach. In fact, 85% of them live within an hour's drive of the coast. People head to the beach to relax, meet friends, swim, sunbathe, snorkel and surf.

Yuraygir beach on a busy day

AUSTRALIA'S BEST BEACHES

Famous beaches such as Bondi (opposite) are ALWAYS crammed. But if you put in a bit of extra effort, it's possible to find less crowded beaches:

Effort level 1: Yuraygir, New South Wales

The 10-km walking trail through this national park takes you past beautiful landscapes and lakes. The way is easily found, but even in the shade it can be a hot walk. The beach itself is great for surfing and fishing: you could catch a few waves, before casting out a line to catch your lunch!

Effort level 2: Bynoe Harbour, Northern Territory

For this one, you need a four-wheel-drive vehicle, stuffed with camping gear. Drive through the bush to reach the clifftops overlooking the natural harbour, and set up camp in time for sunset over the Timor Sea.

Effort level 3: Cox Bight, Tasmania

There are basically three ways to get to the beach at Cox Bight:
• Walk for days, carrying all your gear
• Travel by boat
• Go by plane – if you can find a seaplane, the beach doubles as a landing spot.

THE BATTLE TO BATHE

In the 1800s, swimming in the sea during daylight hours was banned. The authorities thought it was just TOO rude! In 1902, William Gocher was arrested after announcing his plan to swim in daylight off Manly Beach. But a year later, the ban on daylight swimming ended.

Bondi Beach on a quiet day

LEISURE

BEACH SURVIVAL KIT

Things to take to the beach:

Sunscreen: even on overcast days the sun will burn you

Swimming/snorkelling gear: don't forget waterproof sunscreen

Sarong: can be used as a changing robe, towel, beach blanket or sunshade

Water: (at least a litre per person) and food

Fishing gear: why not try to catch your dinner before heading home?

SURFING AUSTRALIA

Sydney surfer

Surfing is one of Australia's national sports. Dripping-wet surfers carrying boards are a common sight everywhere. It's easy to rent a board if you don't have your own, and the sea is rarely cold enough for you to need a wetsuit – except off the south coast in winter. But where are some good spots for a traveller to check out the waves?

1 BEGINNERS
Manly or Freshwater Beaches, Sydney

The long sandy beaches are perfect for beginner surfers – and you can grab an ice cream from one of the seafront stores when you're done!

2 INTERMEDIATE
Byron Bay, Queensland

Byron has a wide variety of surf breaks, from the relaxed waves at The Pass to the shark-haunted beach at Tallows.

3 EXPERIENCED SURFERS
Bell's Beach, Victoria

Bell's is probably the most famous surf spot in Australia, and is home to the country's longest-running surf contest, first held in 1961. It's a long walk down the cliffs, and the waves are always bigger than they look.

4 EXPERIENCED SURFERS
The Superbank, Queensland

The longest ride in Australia – maybe anywhere – the wave at the Superbank has been ridden for almost 2 km. **Experienced wave-riders only:** on a good day, half of the world's top surfers are out there.

5 EXPERTS ONLY!
Yallingup, Western Australia

This spot is home to several former world champions, so it's good for star spotting. The waves reach 6 metres or higher – if you're looking for a more relaxed time, there's great snorkelling and swimming in the sheltered lagoon.

1 IN 10

Australians are surfers

Number of surfers:
2.5 million

Surf clubs: 236

CRAZY SURF-SPOT NAMES

The surf breaks near Bell's Beach in Victoria have some crazy names:

Winki Pop   **Boobs**   **Steps**

LEISURE

Warm waves at Freshwater Beach, Sydney

Duke Kahanamoku, the first surfer in Australia

SURFING AND SHARKS

During the last 50 years, 53 people have died in shark attacks in Australia. How do you avoid being next?

• Never surf at dawn or sunset

• Avoid murky water, river mouths and channels in reefs or sandbanks

• Never surf if you are bleeding

AUSTRALIA'S FAVOURITE SPORTS

Considering how few people live there, Australia is one of the most successful sporting nations in the world. It must be one of the best places in the world to go and see top-class competitions. So, where are the best places to join the sports-mad crowds?

RUGBY

Most popular in:
New South Wales, Queensland, Australian Capital Territory

Good places to watch:
ANZ Stadium (Sydney), Suncorp Stadium (Brisbane)

Australia has top international teams in both rugby league and rugby union, but league is more popular. In fact, in 2009 it was the most-watched sport on Australian TV.

SWIMMING

Most popular in:
all states

Good places to watch:
Gold Coast Aquatic Centre (site of 2018 Commonwealth Games swimming competition), Sydney Aquatic Centre

Swimming is a popular fitness activity with ordinary people, and most towns and cities have excellent pools. The national team has historically been one of the world's best.

SOCCER

Most popular in:
New South Wales, Victoria, South Australia, Western Australia

Good places to watch:
AAMI Park (Melbourne, Sydney Football Stadium, Perth Oval.

At the top of the game are the Socceroos, Australia's national team. There is a 10-team A-League of the best clubs, which includes one from New Zealand. Most neighbourhoods and towns also have their own teams.

AUSSIE RULES FOOTBALL

Most popular in:

Victoria, Western Australia, South Australia, Tasmania, Northern Territory

Good places to watch:

Melbourne Cricket Ground, Patersons Stadium (Perth)

The ball looks like a rugby ball, you try to score goals like in football... Aussie Rules is difficult for a visitor to understand. Watching a big AFL game is still exciting, though.

CRICKET

Most popular in:

all states and territories

Good places to watch:

Melbourne Cricket Ground, Adelaide Oval

Cricket is played and watched all across the country, and is often called Australia's national sport. It's so popular that in 2010–11, 93.6% of Australians watched some sort of cricket on TV.

TENNIS

Most popular in:

all states

Good places to watch:

Melbourne Park

Australia is home to some of the world's top players, including Novak Djokovic and Jelena Dokic. The Australian Open is one of the world's biggest tournaments, and attracts the game's top stars. There are also great public courts in most big cities and towns, which visitors can use for a small fee.

Aussie Rules football

Beach cricket, Tallows Beach, Byron Bay

AUSSIES LOVE CARS

Summer festival for customised cars

Australia is one of the only countries in the world that can rival the USA for its love of cars and other automobiles. Whether it's racing, fixing, customising or simply looking at them, Aussies – especially Aussie men – just LOVE cars.

THE GREAT RACE

If you want to experience Australia's love of cars first hand, head for the town of Bathurst in early October. Normally, Bathurst is a small city of about 30,000 people. For the first Sunday in October, though, its population swells to over six times that size. The crowds are here to see 'The Great Race': the Bathurst 1000.

The race happens on a 'street circuit' – a racetrack that is usually a public road. The cars are V8 Supercars, which are based on cars you can walk into a showroom and buy (if you have a driving licence and lots of money). On the fastest part of the circuit they reach speeds of 300 kph. Each car has two drivers, who take it in turns to rest and drive for the six hours or more of the race.

Bathurst 1000

"We need a vehicle to go to church on Sunday, and which can carry our pigs to market on Monday."

— a farmer's wife writes to a car company in 1932: her letter led to the first ute being built

THE UTE

'Ute' is short for 'utility', which means usefulness. A ute is a kind of Australian vehicle: the front half is a car, the back half is a pick-up. Utes are very popular in Australia, especially in rural areas. People customise their utes, and get together to show them off at 'ute musters'.

FIVE TOP AUSTRALIAN ROADS

1. Great Ocean Road (Victoria)

The road winds along the coast with the ocean to the south, sometimes so close you feel you could fall in.

2. Birdsville Track (South Australia)

Crosses the Tirari and Sturt Stony Deserts, described by explorer Charles Sturt as 'a desolate region having no parallel on Earth'.

3. Gibb River Road (Western Australia)

You need an off-road vehicle for this 700-km trail, which crosses a landscape of red soils, ghost gums and paperbark trees.

4. The Huon Trail (Tasmania)

This circular route shows off the best of Tasmania, including winding rivers, steep mountains and thick, ancient forests.

5. The Fleurieu Peninsula (South Australia)

Some people will tell you this route near the city of Adelaide passes through Australia's most beautiful scenery. The hills roll down to a series of wonderful-looking bays, and the sea is a deep greeny blue.

CAR CULTURE

ABORIGINAL AUSTRALIA

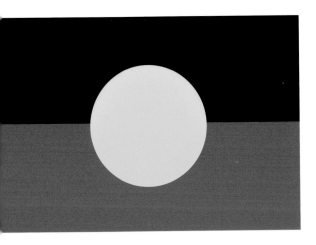

On 26 January each year, Australia Day celebrates the 1788 arrival of the First Fleet, bringing people from Europe. But there were already people living in Australia when the First Fleet arrived. Today, their descendants are known as Aboriginal or Indigenous Australians.

AUSTRALIA DAY V. INVASION DAY

Today, some people prefer to call Australia Day by a different name: Invasion Day. The arrival of Europeans was a disaster for Aborigines. Many died of disease or were killed: by 1900, there were 10–20% as many Aboriginal Australians as in 1788. The survivors lost their land to Europeans.

An Aboriginal guide shows a termite mound to tourists

"If Australia is The Lucky Country, the Aborigines must be the unluckiest people in the world."

— Frank Hardy, Australian writer

ABORIGINAL AUSTRALIA TODAY

Today, many Aboriginal Australians have hard lives. They live an average of 17 years less than other Australians, have lower incomes, worse health and are more likely to be unemployed. But things are improving. There are successful Aboriginal artists, politicians, musicians, lawyers, actors and sportspeople. Aboriginal culture is valued, and the government is taking greater responsibility for ending discrimination against its Aboriginal citizens.

Pop star Jessica Mauboy, whose mother is an Aboriginal Australian

ABORIGINAL FESTIVALS

These are good places to experience traditional Aboriginal culture up close:

BOOMERANG FESTIVAL (Byron Bay, Queensland, October)

Listen to storytellers beside a campfire, learn how to make traditional crafts (boomerang workshop, anyone?) and sit in on the song circles or join the youth camp.

WALKING WITH SPIRITS (Northern Territory, July)

Once a year, the Wugularr Aboriginal people invite members of the public onto their land. There, camping deep in the bush, you can watch traditional ceremonies and performances. Places are limited and tickets sell out very quickly.

YALUKIT WILLAM NGARGEE (Melbourne, February)

This festival's name means 'People Place Gathering', which is a good description of what happens. It's part of the larger St Kilda Festival, and is a great place to see Aboriginal music, dance and other performances.

ABORIGINAL AUSTRALIA

ULURU AND THE RED CENTRE

Uluru

Right at the top of the must-see list for visitors to Australia is Uluru. This giant sandstone rock (also sometimes called Ayers Rock) lies at the centre of the country.

TO CLIMB OR NOT TO CLIMB?

Uluru is an important site for the Anangu Aboriginal people. The Anangu do not climb the rock, and ask that other people don't either. Many tourists do still climb Uluru, however. When they get to the top, many visitors realise that they're standing ON TOP OF the most amazing sight for hundreds of kilometres – so they can't actually SEE it.

The best view of Uluru is from a few kilometres away. Take a picnic in time for sunset, when the sandstone lights up a fiery red colour, and you'll understand why this area of Australia is known as the Red Centre.

ULURU FACTS

Age: 600 million years
Height: 348 m (the top is 863 m above sea level)
Length/width: 3.6/1.9 km
Circumference: 9.4 km

Like an iceberg floating on the sea, Uluru is actually the tip of a much bigger landform, most of which lies underground. Exactly how far down the rock stretches is not known, but it is thought to be several kilometres.

The Devil's Marbles

Wave rock

FOUR MORE NATURAL WONDERS

Uluru is far from the only natural wonder in Australia. Here are four more:

The Great Barrier Reef (North East coast)

Stretching for 3,000 km off the coast of Queensland, the reef is a paradise for snorkelling and diving.

The Devil's Marbles (Northern Territory)

This collection of giant red boulders (called Karlu Karlu by the Aboriginal people) is believed by some to be the fossilised eggs of the Rainbow Serpent, a creature from Aboriginal myths.

Wave Rock (Western Australia)

A 14-metre-high wall of rock shaped just like a breaking wave – a great place for surfers to pose for joke photos!

The Three Sisters (New South Wales)

These peaks overlooking a deep, wide valley get their name from an old Aboriginal story. Three sisters were turned to stone for their own protection – but the man who cast the spell was then killed in a battle. The sisters were stuck, and stand there to this day.

INDIGENOUS AUSTRALIA

DEADLY CREATURES OF AUSTRALIA

As far as the deadly creature count goes, Australia must be one of the most dangerous countries in the world. The countryside, sea, rivers and even the cities are all home to animals that can kill you.

TOP KILLERS

These were the Australian animals that caused the most human fatalities between 2000 and 2010. They may not be what you expect!

1. Horse/pony/donkey (77 deaths)
2. Bull or cow (33 deaths)
3. Dog (27 deaths)
4. Kangaroo (18 deaths)
5. Bee, shark (16 deaths each)

13-year-old Hannah Mighall shows the results of a shark attack

SEVEN MOST DEADLY

This top seven most-deadly animals includes the ones you should work REALLY hard to avoid.

1. The Box Jellyfish

Found in the seas off the northeast coast, this creature is often claimed to kill more people than any other. It is almost impossible to see, so swimmers must wear protective full-body suits for protection.

Saltwater crocodile

2. Saltwater Crocodile

The 'saltie' lurks underwater waiting for prey. When something edible – a tourist, for example – appears, it leaps out and drags it under. Found in the sea and fresh water, they even chase people across land.

3. Stonefish

Found in Indo-Pacific waters, the stonefish is practically impossible to spot on the sea bottom – until you step on one of its venomous spines. Do this and you'll probably be dead within two hours.

4. Redback Spider

Redbacks love to creep into shoes at night, or lurk under toilet seats, which can make for an unpleasant morning experience. If a redback does bite you, hope it's a male: only the females have venomous bites.

5. Coastal Taipan

Not QUITE as venomous as its inland taipan cousin, but more aggressive when cornered. Its venom can easily kill a grown man.

6. Great White Shark

Common off the coasts of western, southern and eastern Australia – so basically, anywhere you might go surfing. People do survive attacks by great whites ... but it doesn't happen very often.

7. Blue-ringed Octopus

There is no anti-venom for a blue-ringed octopus bite, which paralyses all your muscles and stops your breathing. If artificial respiration is carried out for several hours, the venom breaks down and the victim starts to breathe again. If not, he or she dies.

NATURE AUSTRALIA

THE RAINFOREST

Pristine rainforest along the Bird River, Tasmania

You might not immediately think of rainforest when you think of Australia, but there is plenty of it here. In the southeast there's temperate rainforest, and in the northeast lies tropical rainforest. One of the best places to walk in a rainforest is Tasmania.

CLIMBING MT MURCHISON

Mt Murchison is in the Tarkine, a temperate rainforest (the world's second largest) in northeast Tasmania. Climbing the mountain is challenging, but very beautiful. The trek starts in the rainforest, winding through thick trees and undergrowth. There are species of animals here that don't exist anywhere else, such as the Tasmanian Devil. Watch out for snakes, though!

As you climb higher, the scenery changes. First, you pass through grassland. Then the plants disappear, and the trail climbs up through rock fields, getting steeper and steeper. Finally, you scramble up a rock slope to the crest – and that's when you get a surprise. The top of the mountain is hollow, and down at the bottom of the crater are dark, deep-looking lakes. A nice place to dangle your feet and cool them down!

LOGGING

Logging is a controversial subject in Tasmania. Loggers and their supporters believe that they bring much-needed jobs and money to the island. Environmentalists believe that the natural habitat should be preserved for future generations of people and animals.

An anti-logging protester looks out at cleared forest, Tasmania

TOP RAINFOREST AREAS

DAINTREE (Queensland)

Things to do: sleep in the treetops, go bush-tucker tasting with an Aboriginal guide, take a cruise on the Daintree River

KAKADU (Northern Territory)

Things to do: view Aboriginal rock art, take a crocodile-spotting river cruise, walk to the 250-metre-high Jim Jim Falls

KIMBERLY (Western Australia)

Things to do: go on a wildlife trek looking for rare frogs, toads and the rare northern quoll. A quoll is a little bit like a large, pointy-nosed mouse*.

*Northern quoll trivia: all quolls come from single-parent families, because male quolls die after mating.

GONDWANA RAINFORESTS (New South Wales/Queensland)

Over 50 separate parks contain the world's largest area of sub-tropical rainforest, with an incredible variety of plants and animals. The area around Mt Warning/Wollumbin* is particularly good for bushwalking.

*Trivia: Mt Warning is the first place in Australia to be hit by the sun's rays each day.

NATURE AUSTRALIA

OFFSHORE ISLANDS

There are over 8,000 islands off the coast of Australia. They range in size from tiny uninhabited specks of land (which you can still visit by boat for a picnic lunch or a fishing expedition) to Tasmania, by far the largest.

Hikers at Tasmania's Cradle Mountain and Dove Lake

TOP TIPS FROM TASMANIAN LOCALS

There's plenty to do in Tasmania. Here are five top tips from Tassie locals:

1. Cross the bridge over Cataract Gorge

When there has been heavy rain, it's easy to see how the crashing Tamar River cut this deep gorge through the surrounding hills.

2. Camp at the Bay of Fires

The bay was named for the fires of Aboriginal people on the shore. Free camping is allowed in many areas: you'll wake up to an unforgettable view.

3. Climb The Nut

The Nut is an ancient plug of volcanic material, towering 143 metres above the village of Stanley. A steep path leads to amazing views from the top.

4. Visit Port Arthur

Port Arthur was a penal colony, and is a chilling place to imagine what life was like for people sent here as a punishment.

5. Go penguin spotting

Penguins come ashore at night in lots of different places on Tasmania – Bruny Island is a good spot to see them.

Port Arthur

Penguin spotting

OTHER ISLANDS

LORD HOWE ISLAND

Lying 600 km off the east coast of Australia, this is a great place to get away from modern life. The bicycle is the best way to get around, and there's no mobile phone reception!

DAMPIER ARCHIPELAGO

Named after William Dampier, one of the first Europeans to set eyes on Australia. The sea is rich in wildlife: you can snorkel with dugongs and dolphins, and between July and September, humpback whales may be seen.

TORRES STRAIT ISLANDS

Lying between Australia and New Guinea, the Torres Strait Islands blend the native cultures of both. Famous for their beautiful beaches, only 17 of the 274 islands are inhabited.

AWAY FROM THE MAINLAND

KEY INFORMATION FOR TRAVELLERS

LANGUAGE

English is spoken throughout the country. In some cities there are communities speaking Chinese, Greek, Arabic and other languages.

ENTERING AUSTRALIA

All visitors to Australia must have a visa. New Zealanders are able to get these on arrival, but everyone else has to apply beforehand. Visitors from the UK, USA, Canada and 29 other countries can do this online, via a scheme called the Electronic Travel Authority.

GETTING AROUND

Australia is the size of Western Europe, or the 48 contiguous states of the USA. Travelling from place to place often involves big distances, and to get from city to city, many people fly. There are several low-cost airlines. Trains also run between some cities: the different companies are allied in a group called Rail Australia (www.railaustralia.com.au).

Within cities or local areas, many people use cars, and traffic jams are common at busy times. Trains, buses or trams are good ways to travel shorter distances.

If you want to cycle in Australia, wear a helmet: this is one of the few countries in the world where it is a legal requirement. The busy roads and stressed-out drivers may make it best to stick to marked cycle routes and back roads, unless you are a confident rider.

Taking a tram beats the Melbourne traffic

HEALTH

Australia has agreements with the UK, Republic of Ireland, New Zealand, Sweden, Netherlands, Finland, Belgium, Norway, Slovenia, Malta and Italy that allow citizens of those countries cheaper (and sometimes free) treatment for some medical problems. However, even these agreements do not always provide free healthcare, so it is best to have travel insurance.

POSTAL SERVICES

The national post service is called Australia Post. You can buy stamps at post offices (which are in towns and cities, and some smaller settlements), in hotels and guesthouses, and at some newsagents. Post offices are open 0900–1700 Monday to Friday, and some also open on Saturday mornings.

MOBILE NETWORKS

Mobile coverage is good in most towns and cities, but in rural and isolated areas there may be no coverage at all. Using a foreign phone – even on the same network – is expensive, especially for data, so it's important to turn off data roaming. It's possible to send text messages from many public payphones to Australian mobiles.

INTERNET PROVISION

Internet access in Australia is generally good. There are Internet cafés in most towns, cities and tourist hotspots, and Wifi is available in hotels, cafés and restaurants. There are also touchscreen multimedia payphones in Sydney and Melbourne, though they may not allow a full range of Internet access.

PUBLIC HOLIDAYS

Australia has seven national holidays throughout the year, on which many businesses are closed. The date on which some of these are held changes each year:

1 January	New Year's Day
26 January	Australia Day
Good Friday: dates change	
Easter Monday: three days after Good Friday	
25 April	ANZAC Day
25 December	Christmas Day
26 December	Boxing Day

Each individual state can also declare a certain number of holidays. A popular one, observed in most states, is the Queen's Birthday on the second Monday in June.

CURRENCY:

Australian dollar (Aus$1 = roughly £0.70, €0.80, or US$1.00). Currency can be exchanged at some banks, bureau de change, airports and large hotels. ATM cash withdrawal is possible in towns and cities.

TIME ZONE:

There are three time zones in Australia*:
Western Standard Time, which is 8 hours ahead of GMT
Australian Central Time, which is 9.5 hours ahead of GMT
Eastern Standard Time, which is 10 hours ahead of GMT

* In South Australia, New South Wales, Victoria, Tasmania and Australian Capital Territory, clocks are changed to daylight-saving time. This is usually between October and March, but the dates and the amount of change varies by state.

TELEPHONE DIALLING CODES:

To call Australia from outside the country, add 61 to the beginning of the number, and drop the zero.

To call another country from Australia, add 00 and the country code of the place you are dialling to the beginning of the number, and drop the zero.

OPENING HOURS:

Opening hours tend to be different in the city from the countryside, and in different parts of Australia. As a rough guide, most shops open between 09:00 and 10:00, and shut for the day sometime between 18:00 and 19:00. Most are open on Saturdays. In cities, opening hours may be longer, and shops may open on Sundays.

Australian says:	Visitor hears:	Actual meaning:
Ta	Tar?	Thanks
Half your luck	What?	Congratulations
Mug	Something to put a drink into?	Person who can be made a fool of
Ripper	Tearing something?	Great or good
Bushranger	Ah! One I know! A wildlife park attendant.	Outlaw or highwayman
Cut lunch	Sliced up food? Missed the midday meal?	Sandwiches

FINDING OUT MORE

BOOKS TO READ: NON-FICTION

Australia Aleta Moriarty (Franklin Watts, 2013)

Sydney Paul Mason (Evans Brothers, 2007)
Zooming in on the city that attracts more visitors to Australia than any other, this book contains information on how the city is changing, its neighbourhoods, environmental concerns, and much more.

BOOKS TO READ: FICTION

Crow Country Kate Constable (Allen and Unwin, 2012)
This award-winning novel tells the story of Sadie, who is peeved to be moving from the city to the rural Australian town of Boort. But all is not what it seems in Boort, where crows can talk, people can understand them, and Sadie can travel back in time to discover an ancient mystery...

Stories From The Billabong
James Vance Marshall, illustrated by Francis Firebrace (Frances Lincoln Children's Books, 2010)
Add together one of Australia's best-known children's writers and a talented artist from the Yorta-Yorta people, and what have you got? *Stories From The Billabong*, a retelling of Aboriginal stories that's a real treat from start to finish.

Walkabout
James Vance Marshall (1959)
The story of two children stranded in the Outback after a plane crash. They are helped on their journey home by Aboriginal people, the first of whom dies after catching flu from one of the children.

WEBSITES

www.australia.com
This is the official tourist guide to Australia, and is packed with useful information. The 'About' tab lets you scroll down to facts about travelling in Australia, the country's culture and history and landscapes. The 'Explore' tab is great, leading to information about cities, states, special events and a section for youth travellers.

tinyurl.com/26lemh
This link will take you to the CIA (Central Intelligence Agency) web page about Australia. It's quite dry, but crammed full of useful information and statistics.

www.surfingaustralia.com
A great place to find out about forthcoming competitions, places to go surfing, where you can get lessons, Australia's leading surfers and more. Contains state-by-state sections as well as the Australia-wide main site.

Note to parents and teachers:
Every effort has been made by the Publishers to ensure that these websites are suitable for children, that they are of the highest educational value, and that they contain no inappropriate or offensive material. However, because of the nature of the Internet, it is impossible to guarantee that the contents of these sites will not be altered. We strongly advise that Internet access is supervised by a responsible adult.

THE ESSENTIALS

INDEX